SMILE!
How to Cope with Braces

8080

by JEANNE BETANCOURT

Illustrated by Mimi Harrison

 Alfred A. Knopf, New York

For all my students from 1962–1980,
whether they wore braces or not.

THIS IS A BORZOI BOOK
PUBLISHED BY ALFRED A. KNOPF, INC.

Text copyright © 1982 by Jeanne Betancourt
Illustrations copyright © 1982 by Mimi Harrison
All rights reserved under International and
Pan-American Copyright Conventions. Published
in the United States by Alfred A. Knopf, Inc.,
New York, and simultaneously in Canada by
Random House of Canada Limited, Toronto.
Distributed by Random House, Inc., New York.
Manufactured in the United States of America
Book design by Mina Greenstein

10 9 8 7 6 5 4 3 2 1

Library of Congress Cataloging
in Publication Data
Betancourt, Jeanne.
Smile! How to cope with braces.
Summary: General information and practical
advice for people who are having their
teeth straightened. Discusses the causes of
crooked teeth and how to cope with the
problems of wearing braces.
1. Orthodontics—Juvenile literature.
2. Orthodontic appliances—Juvenile
literature.   [1. Orthodontics.   2.Teeth—Care
and hygiene]   I. Harrison, Mimi, ill.
II. Title.   RK521.B47   617.6'43   81-11800
ISBN 0-394-94732-0 (lib. bdg.)   AACR2
ISBN 0-394-84732-6 (pbk.)

Acknowledgments

Thanks to the following people for their help with this book:

Henry Adelson, D.D.S.; Stephen Appel, D.D.S.; Erwin Lubit, D.D.S.; Irving Shuman, D.D.S.

Claudia Brett and orthodontic patients in Boulder, Colorado; Richard Hanley and students at Edward R. Murrow High School in Brooklyn, New York; campers at French Woods, New York; patients from the N.Y.U. Orthodontic Clinic, New York; students at Packer Collegiate Institute, Brooklyn, New York; and Martha Kuhlman.

Pat Ross; Suzan Smith.

Special thanks to Gerald Borell, D.D.S., for generous and careful consultations, and to Dinah Stevenson for fine editorial work.

And to Nicole Betancourt for inspiring the idea for this book and to Lee Minoff for recognizing and nurturing it.

Contents

Foreword

Smile! is a book for all—young people and their parents, and adults—who are considering orthodontic treatment. The author provides concise, easily understood information needed to select an orthodontist, ask the right questions before beginning treatment, understand what orthodontic appliances are and how they align teeth and jaws, and know how it will feel to wear "braces."

There is too much at stake—health, appearance, time, money, and comfort—to begin orthodontic treatment without first consulting Smile!

Gerald Borell, D.D.S.
Chairman, Department of Orthodontics
New York University, College of Dentistry

To People
Who Have Braces
or Are Getting Them

This book is for you.

Smile! is the book I needed in 1955 when I became the only kid in my school who was called Silver Teeth. It is the book I wish I had had in 1980 when I learned that my twelve-year-old daughter, Nicole, needed braces.

Having braces is an experience shared by millions of kids. It's becoming a ritual of growing up in America. So, in researching this book, I turned not only to orthodontists, specialists in straightening teeth, but also to the other group of experts on braces—people who are having their teeth straightened. They told me how they feel about having braces and how they cope with them. They generously pass their experiences and advice on to you in these pages—in direct quotes and through all they taught me.

Twenty percent of the orthodontic patients in America are adults. If you are among them, these pages are meant for you, too.

Jeanne Betancourt

SMILE!

1. "Why Me?"

We are born toothless. With considerable pain, drooling, gnawing, and crying, we acquire our first teeth. Our twenty baby teeth are in place only a few years before they become loose and fall out one by one. We get a few nickels, dimes, or quarters from the tooth fairy for this trouble, and wait around for the larger permanent teeth to fill in the spaces left behind by the baby teeth. Eventually new teeth grow in. There are thirty-two in a permanent set.

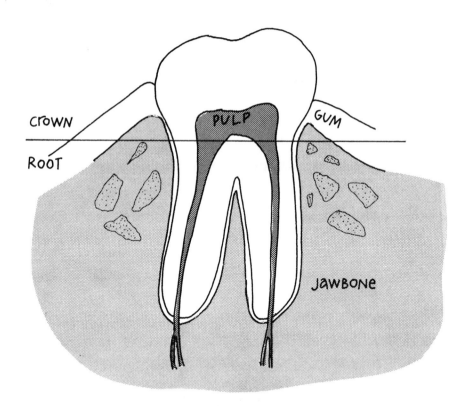

Each tooth consists of a crown, the part you see sticking out from the gum; and a root or roots, the part embedded in the jawbone and gum.

The crown of a tooth has an outer shell of enamel. Enamel is the hardest substance in the body (it is harder than bone), and it has no feeling at all. Dentin, the bonelike substance under the enamel, is very sensitive to temperature and sweets. The pulp, at the center of the tooth, contains nerves. These nerves send pain signals to the brain if tooth decay reaches the dentin or the pulp.

The fibers that connect the teeth to the jawbones are flexible, particularly while our bodies are still growing. That's why even a nonviolent activity like thumb sucking can move teeth forward, and why one tooth can push into another's space and overlap it. The bone that holds the teeth is also flexible, and it can be directed in the way it grows by such forces as tongues, thumbs, and pacifiers.

The fact that bone is pliable explains why teeth and jawbones can be pushed, pulled, and set into corrected positions by dentists with special training. These specialists are called orthodontists, and the kind of dentistry they practice is called orthodontics. (The words "orthodontist" and "orthodontics" come from Greek words that mean "straight teeth.")

Orthodontic appliances—usually called braces —are the tools that do the work of straightening teeth. Metal bands, brackets, wires, rubber bands, and other appliances are attached to the teeth. The orthodontist uses these braces to move teeth and/or to encourage the growth of jaws to the position that is healthiest and most attractive for each patient.

If your teeth are significantly crooked, if your upper and lower jaws don't meet correctly, you may find yourself at the orthodontist's—along with millions of other kids and adults. According to a survey by the American Council on Education, one out of every two school-age children could benefit from orthodontic treatment. The same survey tells us that one out of every five school-age children has a severe orthodontic problem. So it isn't surprising that you need braces.

WHAT'S WRONG?

To make it easier to talk about orthodontics, the dental profession divides the human "bite" and the related placement of teeth into classes. (Your "bite" is simply the way your teeth and jaws come together when the teeth are closed.)

Normal Occlusion

The term "occlusion" is derived from the word "occlude," meaning to close or shut. Normal occlusion—a normal bite—is what everyone

wants. It should be the end result of your orthodontic treatment. A normal occlusion is straight,
well-spaced teeth in normal jaw relationship,
based on the position of the first molars. (Those are
the first wide teeth in the back.) The upper and
lower first molars fit together like the pieces of a
puzzle.

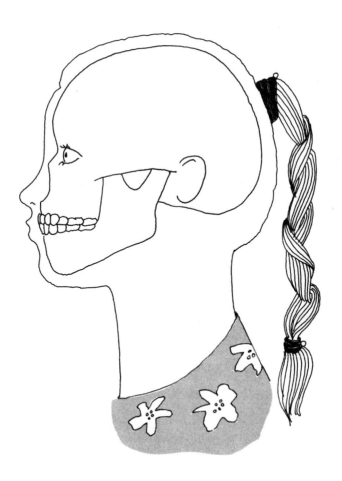

Class I Malocclusion

Remember, "occlude" means to close or shut; but, alas, "mal-" means badly. So, a malocclusion is a "bad bite," one that isn't normal in some way. If you have a Class I malocclusion, your first molars fit together in the proper jaw relationship, but you have crooked teeth or some other orthodontic problem. Your incisors (front teeth) might overlap. Or your canines (the pointed "Dracula" teeth) might be crowded out of line by the molars.

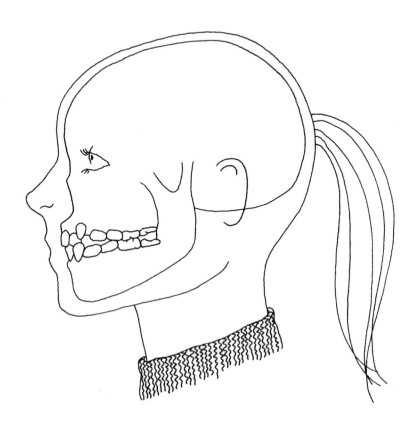

Class II Malocclusion

After Class I come the genuine "bad bites" or malocclusions. Class I malocclusions are not too serious, though they may be unattractive; Class II (and Class III) malocclusions are more serious, because the relationship of the jaws isn't normal. In Class II, the upper first molar is half a tooth or more ahead of the lower first molar when the teeth are closed or come into full contact. This may cause the upper front teeth to stick out over the lower ones. Think of Bugs Bunny.

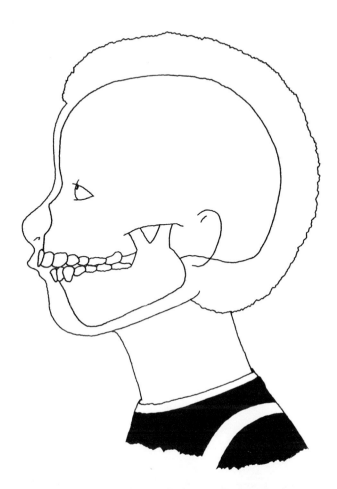

Class III Malocclusion

A Class III malocclusion is just the opposite of a Class II. The upper first molar is half a tooth or more *behind* the lower first molar. The lower jaw juts out noticeably. Think of Dick Tracy.

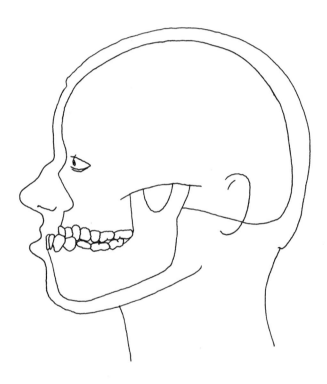

Within each of the three classes there can be other orthodontic problems related to the malocclusion. You might have:

Crowded teeth. Teeth become crowded when there is not enough room in the jaws for all of them. They might be too tightly spaced and/or overlap.

Missing or extra teeth.   Some people have teeth missing, which can cause uneven spacing of remaining teeth; others have extra teeth, which can cause crowding.

Open bite.   You have an open bite if your incisors (front teeth) don't meet because other teeth, farther back in your mouth, hit first when you close your mouth. If you have an open bite you can never close your mouth completely. An open bite interferes with chewing food properly.

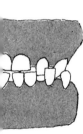

Closed bite.   This is just the opposite of an open bite—the mouth closes too much, so that the teeth of the smaller jaw (whether upper or lower) hit the gums of the other jaw instead of other teeth. A closed bite can be very uncomfortable for its owner.

Cross bite.   In a cross bite the jaws don't meet properly, but the displacement is side to side, rather than front to back.

"HOW DID IT HAPPEN?"

What went wrong that has caused so many of us, and particularly you, to need braces?

There are many causes for malocclusions. In some cases it's hard to pin the causes down. In other cases they are easy to figure out.

The following explanations account for many orthodontic problems.

Evolutionary Changes

The human body has changed during our evolution from our cave-dwelling ancestors. Over millions of years the human brain has increased in size, taking up more room in the cranium. At the same time, the jaws have become smaller, and the face has become flatter. Bigger brains, daintier faces—sounds fine. But as the jaws became smaller, the number of teeth remained the same. Teeth may have been getting smaller over the centuries, but the jaws have shrunk much faster. It's close quarters for modern teeth. Many of us can trace at least part of our orthodontic problems to this evolutionary slipup.

CLASS OF 2,000,000 B.C.

SABER TOOTH MIDDLE SCHOOL

Thumb Sucking

Thumb sucking is responsible for many open bites. Particularly when permanent teeth are coming in, it tends to open the bite so that front teeth don't meet. The constant pressure on the roof of the mouth and against the front teeth is surprisingly powerful. If you continue to suck your thumb during and after orthodontic treatment, you can completely counteract the effect of your braces.

Tongue Thrusting

Tongue thrusting is pushing the tongue against or between the front teeth, usually to aid in swallowing. If you breathe through your mouth, you need to thrust your tongue between your front teeth in order to swallow. (Try swallowing with your jaws open and see!)

If you have an open bite, you will probably breathe through your mouth. And if you breathe through your mouth you will thrust your tongue, which may gradually push your front teeth outward, producing an open bite. It is generally impossible to tell which came first, the tongue thrusting that opened the open bite, or the mouth-breathing caused by an open bite, which leads to tongue thrusting. (This gets orthodontists confused, too.) The point is that the tongue is a powerful muscle that beats against the front teeth of a tongue thruster at the rate of two times a minute—which could add up to 2,880 times a day, 1,051,200 times a year! This is a mighty force—so mighty that if a person continues to tongue thrust during or after treatment to correct an open bite, the orthodontic treatment won't work.

Mixed Heredity

Does your mother have big teeth while your father has a small mouth? And did you inherit a small jaw from your dad and big teeth from your mom? That's mixed heredity. Mixed heredity is the cause of many orthodontic problems. Of course, you can also fault just one side of the family, as in, "You have buck teeth—just like all your father's relatives."

Dental Problems

A dental problem, like early loss of baby teeth, can result in an orthodontic problem. For example, if a decayed baby tooth falls out or is removed before the permanent tooth is ready to replace it, teeth on either side may lean into the space. Then, when the permanent tooth is ready to grow in, there isn't enough room for it. The result can be an orthodontic problem like crowding, crooked teeth, or overlapping teeth.

You still may not be sure what caused your malocclusion, but you and your dentist are sure you have one. The next step is to decide what to do about it.

"DO I REALLY NEED BRACES?"

Some orthodontic problems can and do go untreated, and no one is the worse for it. (I'll say more about this in a moment.) However, some malocclusions should be corrected to prevent other difficulties from developing, particularly later in life. These unpleasant problems *could* include:

Fractured teeth. Protruding teeth, unprotected by lips, can be broken easily if you are hit in the face by a baseball—or by a fist, a sidewalk, a door, etc.

Speech problems. Irregular placement of teeth and imperfect bite can interfere with getting the right sounds out when you talk.

Gum problems. Incorrect alignment of teeth can cause deterioration in the gums that support them.

Cavities. Seriously crowded, overlapping teeth are hard to clean properly, and cavities can result.

Digestive disorders. Orthodontic problems can interfere with proper chewing, and thus with digestion. So they may eventually lead to digestive disorders.

Joint problems. The jaws and the muscles that work them may not function properly because of the disharmonious relationship of the jaws. This can produce pain in the left and right joints of the jaw or in the muscles that move the lower jaw.

Not all untreated orthodontic problems will result in such disorders. In many cases, teeth may be improperly spaced or crowded without significantly threatening physical well-being. Many people get braces solely for esthetic or cosmetic reasons—to improve their looks. On the other hand, not everyone thinks it's so important to have perfectly straight teeth. In fact, some people feel that a crooked incisor or a gap in their teeth makes them look distinctive, and they choose to keep it—even though technically it is an "orthodontic problem."

The benefit of orthodontics—especially if it's entirely esthetic—may be outweighed by financial or other personal considerations. It may come down to a choice between a straight incisor and special classes in music or dance, summer camp, or a special academic program. After consulting with an orthodontist, your parents may decide that you should wait and correct your orthodontic problem when you are an adult. This is more likely to happen if early treatment isn't important in your case or if the orthodontic problem isn't too serious. When you are self-supporting, you can join the millions of adults with braces!

So many kids wear braces these days that a few kids I met said they felt left out because they *don't* wear them. Some kids even push their parents to "give them" braces. And some parents might want to have their child in braces as a visible sign of affluence, a way to tell the world that they've "made it." These attitudes may make you feel better about having braces if you've been concentrating on how awful it is, but by themselves they are *not* good reasons to get braces.

Orthodontic treatment is costly, inconvenient, and time-consuming. You should know why you need it before you begin. You should find out what difference the treatment will make to your dental health, to your general health, and to your appearance *before committing yourself to treatment.* Then you should go into it because *you* want it.

"WHY NOW?"

Most orthodontic work is done on patients in their preteens and early teens. "Why?" you very well might ask. "Why now, just when I really care about how I look? Why not when I was seven or eight and didn't notice if my clothes were five days dirty or if I never combed my hair?"

Well, as you've probably observed, orthodontic treatment *is* done at all ages. And indeed some problems, if caught at the age of six or seven, can be treated more easily than they would be later on. But most problems are best treated after the permanent teeth have come in and before the bony jaw structure has completed most of its growth. Girls reach this stage of dental development at around age eleven, and boys at around age thirteen. At about these ages, girls and boys will usually begin a period of rapid growth. This is a time when it is fairly easy to guide the growth of the jaws and teeth with orthodontic appliances.

2. Getting Started

CHOOSING AN ORTHODONTIST

Who will be your orthodontist? How will you decide?

If there is only one orthodontist in your city, town, or rural area, he or she will be the one you are blessed or stuck with. When I started my treatment in 1955 there were only two orthodontists in the state of Vermont. In 1980 there were fourteen.

Many people entering treatment today can choose among two or more orthodontists. It makes sense to *select* your orthodontist, if you can. We are careful—or try to be—about who fixes the television set or cuts our hair. Equal care should be taken in choosing an orthodontist. After all, this person will be roaming around in your mouth with any number of weird gadgets for a couple of years, maybe longer. The orthodontist may, in effect, reshape your profile, determining how you will look for the rest of your life.

Many people are told by their regular dentist that they should consult an orthodontist—advice the person often confirms by looking in the mirror or confronting a tough steak. Dentists, of course, know lots of other dentists, and usually refer their patients to a local orthodontist.

A person with braces still has to go to a regular dentist for ordinary dental work—for cleanings, to have fillings put in, and so forth. Your dentist probably treats orthodontic patients, so he or she is in a good position to judge a local orthodontist's work.

Your orthodontist may be a woman. In 1980 the American Association of Orthodontists estimated that two hundred of the seven thousand orthodontists in the United States (fewer than 3 percent) were women, and that about 5 percent of the orthodontists then being trained were women.

When your dentist, or anyone else, recommends an orthodontist, you should find out:

How long this person has known the orthodontist and his or her work.

What this person has observed about other patients who are treated by the orthodontist.

Why this person thinks the orthodontist would be a good one for you.

What other local orthodontists this person would recommend, and why.

Try to talk to people who have been in treatment with the orthodontist you are considering. Ask them how they feel about their treatment. Ask them about the orthodontist's attitude toward his or her work and patients.

CLINICS

Dental schools of orthodontics run clinics for orthodontic treatment. Orthodontists-in-training are graduates of a school of dentistry. They're *real* dentists. They need patients to practice on while they learn the specialty of orthodontics. Many people have their orthodontic work done in these clinics.

Here are some things you should know about clinics associated with graduate programs of orthodontics:

They are not charity clinics for people who can't afford orthodontics. Your family's income has nothing to do with whether the school will accept your case or not. Patients are accepted for treatment because their cases have special teaching value. You have to apply. Your "problem" must fit in with what the school needs as case studies for the students.

Your case does not have to be unusual. Often the most common and easily treated problems are in demand.

You may be put on a waiting list or rejected because the school has enough cases like yours at the time you apply. Don't take it personally.

Cases in progress at a clinic are carefully monitored as orthodontists-in-training are supervised and evaluated by their teachers. You will get loads of attention from lots of dentists.

The treatment and the individual sessions may last longer because of the "training" aspects of the program.

Dental schools keep school hours, so your appointments are apt to fall between nine and three o'clock. Some clinics accommodate their patients by having evening hours once a week, or by giving some appointments on Saturday mornings. These are the exceptions.

The total cost of care in a clinic is usually below the cost of treatment with an orthodontist who is in private practice. Sometimes patients save as much as half. Surgical procedures are the biggest "bargain."

Yes, these schools are looking for adult patients as well as kids.

Almost all dental schools have orthodontic clinics. The American Association of Orthodontics can help you locate one in your vicinity.

American Association of Orthodontics
460 North Lindberg Boulevard
St. Louis, Missouri 63141
phone: (314) 993-1700

Before braces are actually put in your mouth, you'll go through a three-step process with the orthodontist: first contact, examination, and consultation. At any point during these early steps, you may decide you don't want to use that particular orthodontist. Or you and your parents may decide that you won't have braces at all—at least for the time being.

FIRST CONTACT

You've been referred to an orthodontist. It's time for your first contact with his or her office. The main point of the contact is to make arrangements for an examination. Some people want to see the office and the doctor in person before committing themselves to the examination. Others do this step by phone. If you do it in person, the orthodontist may look at your mouth and jaw. But you won't be given much information about proposed treatment until after your examination.

An orthodontist's office looks like a regular dentist's office. You'll recognize the big chairs that tilt back, the overhead lamps, X-ray machines, cabinets for instruments, and sinks. Some orthodontists have more than one treatment chair to a room. This may make your visits to the orthodontist more social than visits to your regular dentist.

Just about every orthodontist has at least one dental assistant. These are the people who keep things running smoothly in the office and do a lot of the work apart from the actual treatment. They assist the orthodontist during individual sessions, getting materials and tools as they are needed. A dental assistant needs to understand orthodontics, particularly the vocabulary that describes the instruments and materials. Some assistants participate in a one-year training program to prepare them for this work. Others are completely trained on the job.

Your orthodontist may also have a receptionist who takes care of the appointment book and other office details. In a small office the dental assistant may also do this receptionist/secretarial work.

THE EXAMINATION

Your initial examination will last about an hour. The orthodontist and his or her staff take X rays and photographs, and make a plaster study cast of your teeth. These will help the doctor evaluate your case and set up the course of treatment.

The X rays may include cephalometrics. These

pictures show the whole skull with teeth in their relationship to jawbones and other bones of the face.

The plaster study cast is an exact model of your teeth. Having the mold for the plaster model made is not painful, but it is an unusual experience, and you should be prepared for it.

Step one. Two metal trays are chosen, one to fit each of your jaws.

Step two. The dental assistant mixes a powder with water to form a mixture that is about the consistency of pancake batter. This is done at the counter, not in your mouth!

Step three. Some of this mixture is placed in the metal tray that fits your upper jaw, and then the tray is put in your mouth—against the roof and around the teeth. In less than a minute the mixture becomes rubbery, like a gelatin dessert. It does *not* become hot or hard. It is removed. The same thing is then done with the lower jaw.

Look at the two metal trays after they come out of your mouth. You can see the impressions made by your teeth, and the shape of the inside of your mouth.

After you've gone home, the assistant will put plaster into the molds. It hardens and is removed. Now the orthodontist has plaster models of your teeth.

The initial examination costs money. You should know how much. If you choose to go into treatment, the cost of the examination may be part

"My orthodontist makes a good impression!"

of the total fee. If you don't, it's a separate fee. The photos, X rays, and study casts are expensive. They're also *yours*, so if you decide to consult a different orthodontist, you should take them along. This will save you money, time, and repeated work.

THE ORTHODONTISTS' COMPUTER

Every case is unique. Because individual growth patterns and response to treatment are not completely predictable, your orthodontist can't say your case will turn out just like Patient X's. At the same time, there are similarities and patterns in patient histories that orthodontists can use in analyzing a case. When your doctor studies your mouth, X rays, and plaster models, he or she mentally compares your case with similar cases in his or her practice, and in dental books and journals. Some would say that, all other things being equal, the more cases your orthodontist can compare your case with, the more accurately he or she can predict the results of a particular type of treatment.

A computer service started in 1969, the Rocky Mountain Company, stores information on hundreds of thousands of orthodontic cases. An orthodontist using the service provides the computer with information on your case, particularly from your cephalometric X rays. The computer compares these data with what is in the system on other, similar cases. The resulting printout predicts how your teeth and jaws will look in ten years if treatment is done, how they will look if there is no orthodontic treatment, and how you can be expected to respond to specific courses of treatment. This computer system is especially useful in helping orthodontists decide how early they can start treatment with children.

The computer service is a diagnostic tool that some orthodontists choose to use and others do not. As with any computer system, the usefulness of the results depends on the accuracy of the information that goes into it, the intelligence and skill of the programers, and the competence of the orthodontist who uses the service.

THE CONSULTATION

A week or two after the examination, you will have a consultation with your orthodontist. With the aid of your plaster study casts, X rays, and photos, the orthodontist will explain your case and how he or she would treat it.

Sometimes kids are discouraged from going to the consultation—their parents go to it alone. But you should definitely be there. It is, after all, your mouth that is being discussed. If there are things the orthodontist wants to talk about privately with your parents, this can be done before or after the main part of the consultation. Money is the sort of thing the orthodontist might be reluctant to talk about in front of you.

Here are some important points that should be covered in your consultation:

Why you need braces.

What would happen if you didn't get them.

What will be done to correct your problem.

How long the prescribed treatment will take.

Whether teeth will be extracted as part of the treatment—why, when, and how many.

How your appearance—shape of profile, position of lips—will be altered by the treatment, and what choice you have in the way you will look.

How much the treatment will cost, and what the payment schedule will be. (This should certainly be discussed, even if you are not present for this part of the consultation.)

The purpose of the consultation session is to explain your problem and lay out the entire plan of treatment. Be sure you understand the explanations. If you have trouble following the discussion, ask the orthodontist to go over the confusing parts again. Part of the orthodontist's job is to be sure that you know why you need braces and how your case will be treated. Your prospective doctor may have hundreds of patients, but you have only one mouth and one set of permanent teeth. You should understand what your own case involves right from the start.

Orthodontics is a biological science. Orthodontists are doctors of the mouth and its related bone structure. But orthodontics is also a mechanical science—a system of pushes and pulls. There are no great mysteries in it, no magical powers at work. If there is something you don't understand about your case, ask the orthodontist at any time in your treatment. If you have questions, call the office and make an appointment to talk. Or write the questions down so you can ask them at your next scheduled visit.

Some medical professionals have an "ignorance is bliss" attitude toward their patients. They think you are better off *not* knowing what's going on.

Others feel it's beneath them to discuss medical matters with a lay person. Don't let these attitudes intimidate you.

Your orthodontist may even think you don't *want* to know very much. Make it clear that you *do* want to understand what is going on in your own mouth. You have a right to know anything you want about your own case. It isn't an overstatement to say that you have the responsibility to find out what is being done and why.

You can start right in at the consultation showing a responsible interest in yourself. And one important thing to get settled is how you will look after treatment.

"HOW WILL I LOOK?"

In some orthodontic cases, facial appearance is barely changed as a result of treatment; in others, the changes are dramatic.

How will *your* mouth and jaw look when your braces come off? Will your profile be different? How?

Like plastic surgeons, orthodontists may have a choice in the outcome of their work. Different courses of treatment—each equally suitable for correcting your malocclusion—can have different effects on the shape of your mouth and lower facial profile.

A few orthodontists think that everyone wants, or should have, a flat profile. They treat all their patients—Italian, black, Hispanic—so they end up with look-alike mouths and chins. (If these orthodontists were plastic surgeons, their patients would all be given identical little pug noses, too!) But not everyone wants, or likes, primly tucked-in lips and a flat face. If you have wonderful sensual lips that are off-kilter because of buck teeth, you just might want to keep your luscious lips after your bite has been corrected.

Talk with the orthodontist about how your treatment will affect your appearance. Find out if you have a choice about how flat your profile will be, how full your lips, or how prominent your chin. Be sure you and the orthodontist have the same mental picture of how you will look when the job's done.

EXTRACTIONS

In a significant number of cases, first teeth and/or permanent teeth may have to be removed—for example, if there is insufficient room in the jaws for all the permanent teeth, or if there are extra teeth. You may have this work done as the first step or while the treatment is progressing. Usually the orthodontist will refer you to your dentist or to an oral surgeon for these extractions. If extractions are required in your case, the orthodontist should explain why.

3. The Hardware

During your first two or three visits after the consultation, your orthodontist puts on the basic orthodontic appliances—your braces. These first sessions will last about an hour each.

When a new appliance is put in your mouth or an adjustment is made, you should ask what is being done and why. This will help you to understand your own case—which, of course, will help you to follow the orthodontist's instructions correctly and thus make the treatment work as effectively as possible.

It's natural to feel a bit apprehensive at this point, but remember:

Most appliances look worse than they feel.

Appliances are uglier out of the mouth than when they're in place.

Hundreds of thousands of straightened teeth and beautiful smiles have been accomplished with appliances just like yours.

METAL BANDS

Metal bands are the basic appliance in most orthodontic treatments, though they themselves don't move the teeth or change the shape of the jaw.

Before the metal bands are installed, the orthodontist may need to widen the spaces between your teeth to make room for the bands. Separators, little pieces of metal or plastic, do this job. They are left in place for anywhere from a few minutes to a few weeks, depending on how tightly your teeth fit against one another. When the bands have been fitted onto the teeth, the separators are removed.

You may feel a snugness between your teeth when separators or metal bands are put in. This feeling soon goes away.

METAL BRACKETS

You will notice that each band has a little metal bracket welded onto the front of it. The appliances that move the individual teeth and change the jaw relationship are attached to these metal brackets.

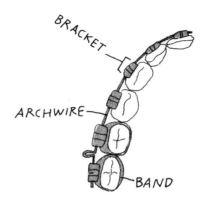

The tooth with a band and bracket on it isn't necessarily going to be moved, but may be used to help other teeth move.

Sometimes metal brackets can be bonded (glued) directly to the teeth. Our space-age technology invented the glue that makes it possible for brackets to stay on the teeth for as long as necessary and then to come off in a snap when their job is done. The choice between bands and glue depends on how much stress the appliance will have to take as your teeth are straightened. Metal bands supporting metal brackets can take the most stress.

PLASTIC BRACKETS

Now you see them, now you don't. In many cases clear plastic brackets can be used in place of metal brackets for at least part of the treatment. Their use is relatively new. Plastic brackets are bonded to the teeth.

Plastic brackets are not as durable as metal bands with metal brackets, or even as metal brack-

ets bonded directly to the teeth. Ask your orthodontist if they will work for you.

ARCHWIRES

Archwires connect the bands or brackets on the
inner dental arch (the tongue side of the teeth) or
the outer dental arch (the cheek and lip side of the
teeth). The bands or brackets are fitted with hooks
and tracks that hold these wires in place. The
archwires are made of a highly elastic metal—
such as the space-age metal Nitinol—that applies
gentle force to the teeth. During your visits to your
orthodontist, the archwires will be adjusted so that
they gradually move your teeth in the directions
the orthodontist and you want them to go.

Whether the wires are placed on the inner or
outer dental arch depends on your case and the
particular preferences of your orthodontist. Ask
him or her how the archwires will work to correct
your orthodontic problem.

FUNCTIONAL BRACES

Functional braces are completely removable appliances. The basic design is a plastic or metal base
that fits into the mouth. Clasps attached to this
base hold wires and springs that fit around the
teeth. The activator, the most commonly used

functional brace, is a device into which the teeth can bite in only one position. By controlling the bite, the activator removes abnormal muscular influences and retrains the muscles of the jaw to a "better" bite.

Functional braces are particularly popular in Europe; some American orthodontists use functional braces in selected cases or for part of a treatment. The pros and cons of functional braces versus fixed appliances are best weighed by the orthodontist for each case. If, however, a functional brace becomes part of your treatment, be sure you understand how it works and what it will do for you. Your cooperation is particularly important, since you take the brace out and put it in every day.

SPACE MAINTAINERS

A space maintainer is an orthodontic appliance that keeps a space open in the absence of a tooth. For example, if you lose a baby tooth and the permanent tooth isn't ready to replace it, it is

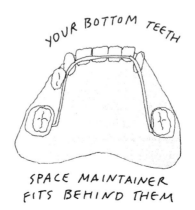

YOUR BOTTOM TEETH

SPACE MAINTAINER
FITS BEHIND THEM

important to prevent teeth on either side from leaning into the space. The space maintainer is usually attached to the tooth next to the space. A bridge of wire goes across the space to the tooth on the other side, or all the way around the inside of the teeth to a tooth on the other side of the mouth. When the new tooth begins to erupt, the space maintainer is removed.

PALATAL SEPARATOR

A palatal separator is an orthodontic appliance that spreads the two halves of the palate (the roof of the mouth). It is used in cases where the upper jaw is too narrow in relation to the lower jaw. The separator fits against the palate and is attached to the teeth on either side. It encourages the two halves of the upper jaw to spread. It is widened gradually, so that the force on the jaw increases gradually. This force is particularly effective when the palate is still growing.

Fortunately, the palatal separator looks worse than it feels.

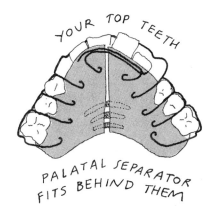

YOUR TOP TEETH

PALATAL SEPARATOR FITS BEHIND THEM

HEADGEAR

Headgear is an orthodontic appliance that goes around the back of the neck or over the top of the head and helps to control the movement of the teeth and the growth of the upper and lower jaws. Headgear has two main parts. First is a strap that

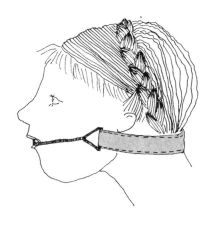

wraps around the top of the head or the back of the neck. The strap is attached to the second part—a bow that fits onto metal brackets on the back molars. Headgear is most often used as part of the treatment for a protruding upper or lower jaw (a Class II or Class III malocclusion).

Usually headgear is not worn twenty-four hours a day. The orthodontist will tell you how many hours you should wear yours. It's likely to be twelve to fourteen hours a day. These headgear hours can pass while you are at home and mostly while you're sleeping.

Not all orthodontic cases need headgear as part of the treatment.

RUBBER BANDS

At some time during your treatment you may wear rubber bands. Rubber bands connecting the two jaws are often used to help correct problems in the bite. In other cases, a rubber band from one tooth to another works effectively at straightening teeth.

Some appliances—like metal bands, brackets, and archwires—are put in your mouth by the orthodontist and there they stay until they are removed. Not so with rubber bands. You put them in and take them out yourself. So, your job is to have your rubber bands in place as many hours a day or night as your orthodontist prescribes. Some orthodontists will tell you to wear rubber bands all the time, explaining that the more you wear them, the faster the job of straightening out the jaw will be done. It depends on your case.

WHAT'S NEXT?

The basic appliances—bands, brackets, archwires, etc.—are in place. The system of pushes and pulls that will bring your teeth and jaws into the desired alignment and adjust their spacing has been set up. You and your orthodontist have begun your course of treatment.

From now on, your orthodontist will want to see you every four to six weeks. These visits will usually last for under twenty minutes. During these sessions your appliances will be checked and adjusted according to the progress of your case. As your teeth and jawbones move, the orthodontist adjusts the archwires and may add other parts to your appliances. During one of the sessions you may be told to wear rubber bands or headgear. You, as well as your doctor, control how fast and how much your teeth move and your bite changes. You can keep the whole process on schedule or slow it down, depending on how well you follow the orthodontist's instructions.

4. Getting Along with Your Orthodontist

Visits to the orthodontist, or any dentist for that matter, make some people very uncomfortable. When the dentists start poking around in their mouths, they are afraid it will hurt. They feel intruded upon, even violated. You may feel this way. Most people do at one time or another. Since the dentist does his or her work in your mouth, it's an understandable and normal reaction.

Think of it. You suckled your first nourishment with your mouth. You communicate by means of your mouth. Life is sustained by the food you eat with it. The breath of life passes through it. The mouth laughs. It cries. It expresses love. It is a gateway to other parts of the body. The mouth is indeed a very important and personal place.

You will feel less intruded upon if you are an active participant in your orthodontic treatment. You can participate by:

Staying calm during sessions.

Working with the orthodontist.

Asking questions.

Understanding what is going on in your mouth.

Most people respect doctors because of their special knowledge and training. That's okay.

Some people have a special awe for doctors and treat them like gods. That's not okay.

It's a big mistake to turn your dental—or medical—problems over to a doctor and then sit back and wait for the "cure" or "miracle."

Your mouth is part of you. It's not like a bike that you leave to be fixed one day and pick up the next all repaired.

Your orthodontic problems are attached to a human being—you. You go with your mouth. You *are* your mouth. The person who cares most about your mouth is *you*. It helps to keep this in mind when you are at the orthodontist's office.

It also helps to keep your sights on the results of your treatment. Since the mouth is important and special, it should be in the best possible condition so it will function at its best. You can't straighten your teeth alone. Your orthodontist is trained and well paid to do it with you and for you. To do his or her part of the job, the orthodontist needs to spend some time in your mouth.

Dentists who choose to specialize in orthodontics know they will be dealing almost exclusively with young people. Most orthodontists enjoy working with kids. Don't be surprised if you find yours is a nice person who understands what you're feeling and goes out of his or her way to help you relax.

Here's what some kids with braces had to say about their orthodontists:

"His stomach growls when you put your head against it."

"He's an old man who knows how to treat kids. He knows how to calm people down. His hands taste like soap."

"He sends cute Christmas cards."

"He always warns me before he does something that hurts me."

"She seems to know what she's doing so I'm not worried she's going to slip."

"He reminds me a little of my grandfather."

"He's not my favorite person but he's okay. He cracks bad jokes."

"I like the fact that he tries to make me feel better about my braces."

"He talks to me nicely while he's working on my teeth. He makes me feel comfortable."

"He tries to be funny and even if he is I can't laugh because he has his hands in my mouth."

"She's nice. She doesn't get mad."

DEALING WITH PROBLEMS

Your orthodontist works for you. Presumably when you and your parents chose this person to do important work in your mouth, you made sure he or she was intelligent, skillful, and up-to-date.

Your orthodontist probably has as many quirks and distinguishing personality characteristics as you find in your social studies teacher, the local grocer, or Aunt Irene. You should be able to deal with those personality differences and manage a working relationship. Cooperation between orthodontist and patient is very important to the progress of each case—and that includes *yours*.

There is nothing unusual about feeling a little tense at the orthodontist's, or even in having trouble getting along with him or her at times.

You are in a patient/doctor relationship, which can make you feel powerless. The orthodontist is an adult and you're a kid, which can interfere with your understanding of each other. Certain kinds of problems tend to crop up in this kind of situation. When you are nervous, the doctor may tease and joke with you, thinking it will make you less anxious; but instead, the teasing makes you more edgy, and might make you embarrassed, too. You may think you are being treated like a much younger child. Or you may think your orthodontist isn't taking you seriously enough. You may feel your questions aren't being answered fully.

If you experience difficulties in your relationship with your orthodontist, be careful not to let the situation turn into a battle. The battleground will be your mouth, and the orthodontist controls all the artillery. If you think of your orthodontist as the enemy, you will waste a lot of energy and experience more discomfort than necessary. You will also spend a longer time in braces and spend more money than you need to. Fighting your orthodontist means working against the progress of your own treatment.

If you are having trouble getting along with your orthodontist, perhaps you should try to make the situation more comfortable. Here's what you might do.

First talk to your parents or friends about the problem and ask them to help you think it through. Talking about the situation will help to put it in perspective, and will help you build your courage for the more difficult next step—talking to the orthodontist.

Be calm and honest when you discuss the problem you have in your working relationship. Don't be angry and accusing. Give your orthodontist room for explanations, and *listen* to them. In many cases the doctor is just being misunderstood, or is misunderstanding you.

Your orthodontist may have some justified complaints about you as a patient, so you may also have some work to do in improving the relationship. Are you acting hostile and prickly? Are you being unresponsive, uncooperative? Are you behaving like a younger child? If you are willing to admit that you might have helped to create an uncomfortable relationship with your orthodontist, one honest talk will most likely improve the situation.

Reaching an understanding that you both can live with is probably easier than finding a new doctor. If things don't improve, you may want to think about changing orthodontists. However, if you live in a small town or rural area where there is only one orthodontist, you may not be able to make a change. This is all the more reason to work at straightening things out.

What if you think you have the rare orthodontist who is sadistic or inappropriately sexual with patients? Talk about your feelings with an adult you can trust. He or she will help you analyze the situation and figure out what can be done about it.

5.   Brace Yourself

"I had an orange for lunch and the pulp was hanging from my front braces for the rest of the day. After that I carried toothpicks to school." That's how David, a fourteen-year-old boy, described his most embarrassing experience with braces. Another kid, Annie, worried that when food got stuck in her braces it began to smell. She now keeps a toothbrush at school and brushes after lunch. These kids are learning how to cope with their braces.

YOUR JOB

We've discussed your orthodontist's job. Now let's look at your part in your orthodontic treatment. You can help the orthodontist straighten your teeth and bite as efficiently, comfortably, and successfully as possible.

Your job is to:

Keep your regularly scheduled appointments.

(An appointment missed only adds time to your treatment—time you will have to make up after you should have been finished with braces.)

Keep your teeth and braces clean.

Avoid fiddling with your braces, which can loosen the wires. (Loose wires could cut or irritate the inside of your mouth or lips.)

Protect your braces from bending, breaking, and coming off by avoiding hard and chewy foods.

Follow the orthodontist's instructions to the letter. This includes wearing rubber bands and headgear for the assigned periods.

RUBBER BANDS AND HEADGEAR

Having to wear headgear and/or rubber bands may seem like adding insult to injury. You may feel they make a bad situation even worse. Because you wear them on your own time, not under the orthodontist's direct supervision, you may be tempted to cheat or just not to bother. How will the orthodontist even know?

Consider this. If your orthodontist prescribes rubber bands and/or headgear, they must be important to your treatment—otherwise why would he or she bother you with them? (By the way, the doctor *can* tell if you don't wear these appliances by the lack of progress in your case, even over a short period of time.) If you "cheat" on wearing headgear or rubber bands, it really doesn't matter to your orthodontist. It *will* matter to you and your parents, because the treatment will take longer, cost more, and perhaps be less effective.

Here are a couple of hints on making headgear or rubber bands part of your daily routine:

Have a special spot where you keep your rubber bands or headgear (or other removable appliances) when you aren't wearing them. Some kids told me that when they remove these "unattached appliances" they put them in an especially handsome box or zipper case and *always* leave it in their bookbag or next to their bed. The box or case keeps the appliances from getting lost or damaged, and serves as a reminder to put them on.

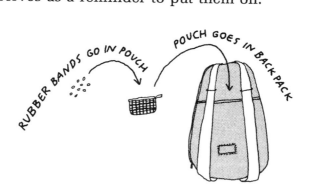

Chart your time. Some people find it helps to keep a record, like a scorecard, of the hours they wear their rubber bands or headgear.

BRUSHING

Brushing teeth with braces on them requires extra care. The area to be cleaned now has all sorts of new crannies where food can sneak in and become wedged, allowing decay-causing bacteria to breed. Your orthodontist may give you a toothbrush especially designed for getting around your braces and into the spaces. If you lose or misplace this brush, just use a regular toothbrush. The orthodontist or an assistant will show you how to brush your teeth after your braces go on.

It's best to brush after every meal. Don't be shy or self-conscious about brushing in the school washroom. It sure beats having food hanging on your braces now, and getting cavities later.

Be sure to give the area between the braces and the gums a good brushing. There are two reasons for doing this. First, food gets caught in this space. You want to get it out so that it won't cause decay. Second, the gums need stimulation to remain healthy. Foods that normally stimulate the gums during chewing are blocked by your braces. Brushing gum areas helps make up for that missing "exercise."

A water squirter for cleaning teeth and gums is fine to use and can be helpful. But brush before using it. Using a water squirter is *not* a substitute for brushing!

LOOKING GOOD

The DO List

- DO brush your teeth and braces often—preferably after every meal or snack.
- DO look in the mirror after brushing to see if any food particles are left behind.

The DON'T List

- DON'T drink grape juice if you have plastic brackets—it stains them.
- DON'T walk around with your hand over your mouth.
- DON'T stop smiling and laughing. Gloria, a fifteen-year-old, put it this way: "Don't change your smile just because you have braces. If you try to smile without showing them, it looks silly."

SORENESS

A few hours after a visit to the orthodontist, you may begin to experience soreness in your mouth and teeth. It may last for anywhere from several hours to a few days. There will be more soreness after some visits, less after others, and none at all after most. Your orthodontist might call this feeling "discomfort." You might call it pain. Whatever it's called, you're the one who has to put up with it.

Soreness is normal if it occurs right after appliances have been inserted, following a regular visit where adjustments are made, or when you first wear headgear or rubber bands.

Your orthodontist will make suggestions on how to cope with soreness. The most common recommendations are:

Rinse your mouth out with half a teaspoon of salt in a glass of warm water, to relieve irritation and reduce swelling.

Eat only soft foods for a day or so. If you are experiencing soreness, strenuous chewing in the sore area only adds to the discomfort.

If the discomfort is extreme or continues beyond five days, call your orthodontist.

A TROUBLESHOOTER'S GUIDE TO BRACES

Here are some things that can cause you difficulty as you go through orthodontic treatment, and some suggestions on how to handle them.

What Can Go Wrong	What to Do About It
Teeth become tender and/or gums are sore	Keep in mind that some soreness is normal. Try the remedies described above, and anything else your orthodontist may suggest.
Lips, tongue, or inside of cheek are irritated	Try to figure out what is causing the problem. If a wire or other appliance is sticking out, press it back into place. If that doesn't work, cover it with wax, cotton, or even sugarless gum. Call your orthodontist.

O U C H!

What Can Go Wrong	What to Do About It
Archwires or other appliances break and/or fall off	Make an appointment to have a repair job. In the meantime, try to push the broken piece back so that it doesn't dig into your gums, lips, or cheek. If a broken piece is loose enough to remove, remove it. Try to cover what can't be removed or pressed out of the way; use wax, cotton, or sugarless gum.

Canker sores	Braces do not cause canker sores. But if you develop a canker sore while you have braces, check to see if your braces are irritating the spot where the sore has developed. If they are, try to eliminate the source of irritation. Again—bend, press, or cover offending appliances. To relieve the discomfort of the sore, try one of the over-the-counter drugs for mouth sores. Rinsing your mouth with warm salt water might also help.

6.   Facing the World

The closest we come to seeing ourselves physically as others see us is in the mirror and in photographs. We care about how we look to others, so we all turn to the mirror many times a day to "check ourselves out."

To most of us, our external appearance is who we are. Changes in our appearance make us feel uneasy for a while. Sometimes the uneasy feeling is positive and exciting—for example, when we get an attractive new hairstyle or realize that we've become taller and stronger. Other times changes in our appearance make us uneasy in a negative way—for example, if skin breaks out in acne, if we have an undesirable weight gain—or, perhaps, if our smiles are suddenly studded with braces.

It's important to remember that changes in how we look do *not* change who we are.

It's true that when you suddenly confront a "braced you" in the mirror, the new look may take some getting used to. Other people will probably become accustomed to you in braces much more quickly than you do—but then your classmates, friends, and family see you face-to-face more often than you see yourself in the mirror.

Many of you are having your teeth straightened in early adolescence—a time when you are going through all sorts of other changes. Physically you may be growing in big spurts. You are (or will be) developing secondary sex characteristics (like breasts in girls, and beards in boys). Your view of the world and yourself may be changing dramatically. You probably have new interests—and new problems.

You may be the kind of person who can take all these changes in stride. But if you aren't, getting braces—on top of everything else—may seem like the final straw. If you try to remember that having your teeth straightened is something you are doing for *yourself,* it will help you cope with your own reaction and the reactions of others.

OTHER KIDS

When you first get braces, some kids may comment on it. Chances are that kids who are nice to you will be nice about your braces, and the class wise guy will tease you mercilessly.

You might as well be prepared for some of the

names you may be called once you've got your braces. Here's a collection from kids with braces:

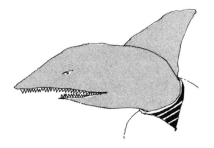

Brace Face
Electric Can Opener
Jailbird
Jaws

Metal Mouth
Motor Mouth
Plastic Palate
Silver Streak
Silver Teeth
Tinker Teeth
Tinsel Teeth
Train Tracks

Michelle told me how a seventh-grade classmate begged to see her removable brace. When she took it out and showed it, the girl said, "Yuck," and told everyone how ugly it was. Paul, a thirteen-year-old, said that his cousin made fun of him by covering his own teeth with aluminum foil.

Most people, kids included, won't really pay much attention to your braces, because these days so many kids and even adults have their teeth straightened. Think about it. How much did you notice other kids' braces before you had your own?

And did it really matter? Would you like or not like a person because he or she wore braces?

Here's one eighth-grader's advice about how to cope with teasing: "Don't be bothered by kids who make fun of your braces. If you didn't have braces they'd find something else about you to pick on." Another junior high school student advised, "Don't make a big fuss about your braces, because if you do, so will everyone else."

If you're upset by being teased about your braces and you let it show, you'll probably just make things worse for yourself. The person doing the teasing may try to provoke the same reaction again and again. Try to ignore the silliness of the people who pester you because of your braces. Everyone will soon tire of their nonsense—including them.

PARENTS

Different parents have different ways of reacting to their children's braces. A few can't handle the situation at all. When it came time for the orthodontist to put the first metal band on one boy, his mother pulled him out of the chair and ran from the orthodontist's office. "You're not using those instruments of medieval torture on my Frank's mouth," she yelled over her shoulder as she stormed out the door.

Another parent made his daughter feel she would be ugly if she didn't have her teeth straightened, and that she should have them straightened *for him.* "Honey, you would look so pretty if you had your teeth fixed. Do it for Daddy." But Daddy had it all wrong. You should only get braces for you—because *you* want to have straight teeth.

Some kids told me their parents baby them too much. The parents think they're helping, but end up making these kids feel worse by reminding them of the ways in which braces are a nuisance.

Still other parents dismiss the discomfort and their kids' complaints with comments like, "Don't complain to me. I have to pay for it, and that hurts me more than what you're feeling hurts you."

If you feel your parents are making it harder for you to get through your orthodontic treatment, try to talk to them about it. Let them know what about their attitude bothers you, but be sure to listen to what they have to say about you. Work it out calmly. Braces shouldn't become a battleground between parents and children, any more than they should between orthodontists and patients.

Remember, even though you are the one who has to put up with the fuss and discomfort, the bottom line is that *you* are the one who ultimately gets the benefits of braces.

WHAT THEY MIGHT REALLY MEAN

We often say one thing but mean another. When people have silly or obnoxious reactions to your braces, this is how they might feel deep down:

"I'm SCARED . . . because my teeth are crooked or might become crooked."

"I'm ENVIOUS . . . because you have something I don't have."

"I'm ENTITLED . . . because people gave *me* a hard time when I had braces; now it's my turn to give you a hard time."

"I'm ANGRY . . . because you make me feel guilty. You're obviously taking good care of your teeth, and I'm not taking good care of mine."

"I'm SAD, or CONFUSED, or UPSET . . . about something else, and I'm taking it out on you."

"HOW DO YOU FEEL ABOUT YOURSELF IN BRACES?"

I asked a lot of kids how braces make them feel about themselves. Thirteen-year-old John answered the question this way: "I feel like a normal teenager—only shinier."

Most kids seem to feel okay about having braces. They're excited about changing their looks and realize the importance of taking care of their dental health. They're willing to put up with the short-term inconveniences for the long-term benefits. As one girl put it, "The greatest thing about having braces is the realization that one day you are going to look different, and that makes you feel better about yourself."

But other kids said they're often upset about the way they look in braces. Some, particularly those over thirteen, said they feel that their braces make them look younger than they are, and they resent them for that reason.

Your feelings about a lot of things are intense and changeable. Maybe one day you don't care and have all but forgotten your braces are there. Another day you think it's terrific to have braces and you can just feel them straightening your teeth right up. And then there are those days when you feel imprisoned by your braces and don't believe you will ever be freed. On those days, say to yourself, "I will wear braces for only a year or two, but I will have straight teeth for the rest of my life." Then quickly get involved in some activity to take your mind off your braces. They'll do the work while you do something else. And remember the words of thirteen-year-old Janice, who said this about her braces: "What difference does it make? Just about everyone else is in the same boat."

7.   You Can Do It

BRACED FOR SPORTS

Braces and sports? Not a problem. Take a good look at Tracy Austin in 1980 when she was winning all those international women's tennis matches. She was wearing braces.

Braces shouldn't limit your participation in any sport. For a rough contact sport like football, wear a mouth guard.

BRACED FOR MUSIC

Do braces interfere with playing a wind instrument? They might if you're a highly advanced concert musician who suddenly has a mouthful of metal. For most musicians, however, playing a wind instrument with braces is not a problem.

But does playing a wind instrument *cause* orthodontic problems, like an open bite? No. Just be sure to develop good *embouchure*—that's the position and use of the lips and mouth in playing a wind instrument. Your music teacher will show you how to hold your instrument in your mouth so that it doesn't put undue pressure on your teeth and palate. The embouchure that protects your teeth is also the one that helps you to produce the best sound.

BRACED FOR EATING

No hard foods, like bagels, whole apples.
No chewy foods, like caramels. No chewing gum.
Cut down on sugar.
Don't chew ice.
No corn on the cob (while it's on the cob!).

So go the commandments for orthodontic patients. These food rules, as obnoxious as they might be to you, do make sense. Some of the "for-

bidden foods" can break and loosen your braces. Others can decay teeth. Some do both. Chewing gum or a sweet, sticky food like caramels can wear away the cement holding braces in place, which loosens the braces and leaves space for food particles to sneak in and cause decay.

The forbidden foods can also add to the discomfort you feel after some appointments with your orthodontist. Strenuous chewing only adds to the soreness, particularly in the hours following the chewing. Be good to yourself and your family by telling whoever does the cooking when you won't be able to eat hard, tough, or chewy foods. The day of an appointment with your orthodontist is a lousy time to have steak. Meat loaf would be a better choice.

The hard part of the food rules for orthodontic patients is that they are so negative—all don't's and no's. Read on to get some do's. Many foods will give you no problem, even on sore-teeth days. You might want to prepare these foods yourself. If you don't intend to be active in the kitchen—and even the food suggestions below can't tempt you to try—share these ideas with the family cooks.

Soft and Smooth Foods

Having to give up a few foods during your orthodontic treatment is a good excuse to try some new foods and new ways of preparing them.

A lot of the foods you eat routinely are naturally

soft and smooth. Some tough, hard foods can be made softer and smoother. Chop! Blend! Cut! Slice! Mash! The secret is to "chew" the foods *before* you put them in your mouth. Cooking also softens many foods, such as apples and carrots.

Breakfast

Most breakfast foods are soft to begin with —eggs, sausages, pancakes, hot cereals, breads, and many fruits.

For variety, how about a milk shake? Here are a couple of variations that taste terrific and are packed with nutrition.

Blend a cup of milk
With a scoop of yogurt or ice cream
Add chopped fruit (berries and/or bananas are great!), and chopped nuts if you like
And honey, molasses, maple syrup, or chocolate syrup (one tablespoon per serving)

For extra nutrition:

Blend a raw egg with the other ingredients. It sounds disgusting but it adds good flavor and texture, as well as great nutrition. And you won't recognize the raw egg. If you don't believe me, make a shake for a friend without mentioning that there's a raw egg in it. He or she will never notice—and when you try one, neither will you!

M-M-M-M-MILKSHAKE!

A Great Anytime Snack

A frozen milk shake makes a terrific snack. Leave the milk shake in the freezer for three to four hours (longer is okay). Small paper cups make good molds. Make a double milk shake, drink half, and freeze half for later—that is, if you can get it into the freezer before someone else in your family gets a taste.

Lunch

The classic American lunch—hamburger and French fries—is a fine, soft-enough lunch on most braced days. But it might get boring if you had it seven days a week.

MIX AND MATCH SANDWICHES

Choose one or more ingredients from both Column A and Column B. Try new combinations for scrumptious variety and adventurous eating.

Column A	Column B
peanut butter	banana (mashed or sliced)
sliced meat	avocado
chicken salad	lettuce
bologna or other sandwich meat	sprouts
	onion slices
sliced hard-boiled egg or egg salad	chopped olives
	cucumber and/or tomato slices
tuna fish	chopped nuts
cottage or farmer cheese	chopped red or green pepper
cheese slices	sesame seeds
hamburger or other meat patty	raisins
sliced meatballs	

Try different breads—whole wheat, pumpernickel, rye, Syrian.

Spread the bread with one or more of the following:

ketchup	butter	spaghetti sauce
sour cream	mayonnaise	yogurt
mustard	salad dressing	

Add a dash of spices or herbs from the cupboard. You might try curry powder, chili powder, dill, oregano—and, of course, salt and pepper.

If you aren't sure a spread or spice will work well with your combination, try a bit on one bite of your sandwich first.

SALADS

The secret of fixing salads for the braced mouth is to chop or slice hard vegetables and fruits into small pieces. A food processor is a big help. If you don't have one, use a little muscle power and get those apples, carrots, and cabbages into slices, slivers, or little chunks.

Mix   vegetables or fruits
With cottage cheese, farmer cheese, cream cheese, or yogurt (these can also be used as a base for a dressing)
Add   raisins, chopped nuts, sesame seeds
And   mayonnaise or salad dressing, and herbs

A nice variation is to toss in chunks of cheese instead of using the creamy cheeses.

Steaming vegetables and then cooling them is another good way to prepare them for salads that won't offend a sore mouth.

Supper

SOUPS

Soups are always easy on the teeth. You can make your own by cooking a cup of your favorite vegetable(s), chopped, with about two cups of liquid—water with a couple of bouillon cubes, canned broth, or homemade stock. Add a quarter of a cup of uncooked noodles or rice, or half a cup of diced potato, and simmer for twenty minutes or so. You'll have a nourishing meal without a chewing challenge.

OMELETTES

An omelette (or a crepe, for that matter) is an envelope for other foods. Ask a cook in your family to show you how to make one. Try vegetables, from asparagus to zucchini, most cheeses, or leftover meats in your omelette. Don't forget to add a dash of your favorite spice.

PASTA

Any kind of pasta (macaroni, spaghetti, noodles, ravioli, etc.) will be kind to your mouth. A quick hot meal that's easy to chew is a quarter pound of spaghetti; a hunk of butter; a bit of sour cream, heavy cream, or milk; and grated Parmesan cheese.

FISH

Fish is soft. If you don't normally include seafood in your diet, maybe this is the time to develop a taste for it.

Here are some kids' suggestions for easy eating with sore teeth:

"Jell-O gelatin."

> "Baby and toddler food for two weeks."
> "Malteds."
> "Apple sauce."
> "Chocolate cream pie with bananas in it!"
> "Mashed bananas with salt."
> "Suck hard foods until they get soft."
> "Cold milk is healthy and it chills away some of the pain."
> "Potato knishes."
> "Chew with your tongue and the roof of your mouth."

BRACED FOR KISSING

Braces don't have to interfere with kissing. Just proceed carefully and gently. If someone wants to kiss you and you want to kiss him or her, you will find a way that is comfortable for both of you.

Here's what kids who have braces said when I asked them, "How do you kiss with braces?"

> "Take off the rubber bands, just to be safe."
> "My braces don't get in the way. You don't kiss with your teeth—right?"
> "I'm only twelve!"
> "Never bothers me!"
> "I don't."
> "It's very difficult and can be embarrassing."
> "You have to overcome your nervousness and work very hard at it."

"It's not that bad if only one of you has braces. You just have to be careful not to get pinched by wires and stuff like that."

"If you're kissing someone else who has braces, you have to be careful that nothing gets caught."

"It's only a pain when they lock."

"It hurts your lips."

"It doesn't bother me because I'm not into kissing. Besides, I'm getting them off in two weeks."

"Brian doesn't mind."

"Be sure no wires are protruding. You don't want to cut up anyone's mouth. It takes a little practice."

"I don't kiss my braces."

8. When Your Braces Come Off

Here's how kids with braces answered the question, "What are you looking forward to most when your braces come off?"

"Straight teeth, a good bite, closed spaces—an overall nice smile."

"Kissing my boyfriend without a bunch of metal in my mouth."

"Looking like a movie star with straight white teeth, like on a commercial for toothpaste."

"Smiling without wondering if food is caught in my teeth."

"A pack of gum and no more bothering about anything."

"Becoming a model. My mother says that as soon as I get my braces off she's going to take me to a modeling agency."

"The reaction of my family and friends."

"Looking my age."

"Having more confidence about my looks."

"Seeing my teeth again."

"Easy brushing."

"Eating a whole pound of chocolate and generally making a pig of myself."

"Less pain and less guilt."

"Biting into an apple."

"Looking at other people and not seeing all that metal reflected in their eyes."

"Running my tongue across my teeth."

SMILE!

When you start treatment, your orthodontist estimates how long it will take. Usually the estimate leaves at least six months of leeway. A typical prediction is, "If all goes well this case will take from two to two and a half years."

For two years you go faithfully to your regularly scheduled appointments, wear your headgear and/or rubber bands, stay away from gum and hard foods, brush regularly. Finally one day your orthodontist peers into your gaping, silvery mouth and says, "Looking *very* good. I think we can take them off at the next visit."

You are definitely on time for your next appointment. Your braces come off in a snap—it's all easier than you expected, and there's no discomfort. The orthodontist makes a second set of impressions of your teeth, as a record of the changes in your case, and then you glide home on Cloud Nine.

You are smiling from ear to ear at school the next day and *nobody notices*. The classmate who gave you such a hard time when you first got braces doesn't notice they're gone. Maybe your best friend doesn't notice. One tenth-grade girl told me even her *mother* didn't notice, and the mother knew her daughter was going for an appointment to have her braces taken off. But *you* notice, and keep checking that bright straight smile in mirrors and store windows.

It's yours, all right. Now it's up to you to decide if it's for keeps.

STAYING IN SHAPE

In almost every case, orthodontic treatment will continue for a while after braces come off. Your straight teeth may need help to keep them on the right track. Once the pressures and pulls of appliances are gone, your teeth could start moving right back into their crooked and undesirable positions. You and your orthodontist can take steps to help bones, muscles, and teeth "remember" their new positions, so that they don't go back to their old ways.

Retainers and positioners are two devices used after braces come off to keep teeth straight and bites corrected. Some cases don't require these devices. Most do. If your orthodontist prescribes one for you, you will wear it for at least a few months, perhaps for as long as two years.

The Hawley Retainer

The Hawley retainer is a piece of plastic molded to the exact shape of the roof of your mouth. It is made on a plaster model of your corrected bite. Wires fit around your straightened teeth to hold the retainer in place. The retainer is often worn continuously, at least in the beginning.

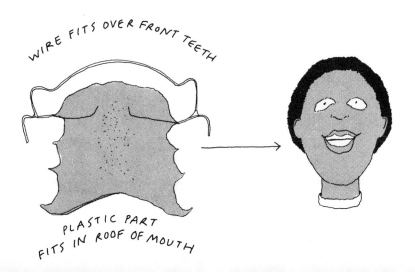

WIRE FITS OVER FRONT TEETH

PLASTIC PART FITS IN ROOF OF MOUTH

The Positioner

The positioner is a rubber mouthpiece molded to fit over your straightened teeth. Positioners are used to finish off the straightening job with precision—pushing the teeth that extra millimeter, encouraging the perfect shape of an arch.

To make the positioner, the orthodontist starts with a new plaster study cast of your teeth. This cast is made toward the end of your treatment. The teeth are cut off this cast and then cemented back on in a *slightly* different position—the finished position for your case. The positioner is made on this ideal study cast. When you wear the positioner, it guides your *almost* perfectly straight teeth into their ideal positions. Because the positioner is rather cumbersome, it is generally not worn full time. In some cases a retainer is used after the positioner.

The orthodontist will tell you to wear your retainer or positioner for a certain number of hours each day and return for periodic visits. Wearing

BITE INTO THESE HOLES!

the retainer or positioner as instructed and return-
ing to your orthodontist for periodic checkups are
your "maintenance program."

As the months go by, you will wear the retainer
or positioner for shorter and shorter periods, and
—finally—not at all. This will happen when your
orthodontist decides your teeth have "learned"
their new positions and probably won't drift anymore. The time between visits to your orthodontist
will lengthen until you go only once or twice a
year, or not at all.

HOLDING THE LINE

During the time you wear braces, people will say
things like, "I bet you'll be real glad when those
things are off." And you'll think, "Gee, I can't wait
to have straight teeth and not have to bother with
this nonsense anymore."

Finally your braces come off. No more metal and
rubber in your mouth. Your teeth are straight. You
look terrific. Then the orthodontist tells you it isn't
over, that you have to wear a retainer or positioner.

But you don't *see* your teeth drifting back into
their old positions. And the retainer or positioner
is a nuisance. So you stick it in a drawer. Out of
sight, out of mind. And your teeth keep drifting.

Not wearing your retainer or positioner can
cancel out much of the time, effort, and money that
you have spent on braces.

Unless you wear your retainer or positioner on

the prescribed schedule, you will find that it becomes increasingly uncomfortable—even painful—to wear. When it is in a drawer instead of in your mouth, your teeth are busy moving back toward their old positions. The retainer or positioner doesn't change its shape. Your mouth and teeth will.

Developing the habit of wearing your retainer or positioner may take some effort. Here are some hints to help you:

Tell your father or mother to ask you periodically whether you are wearing your retainer or positioner.

When you aren't wearing it, put your retainer or positioner in a case. Select a special spot where you'll leave the case when the retainer

or positioner is in it—maybe next to your toothbrush at home, or in a particular pocket of your knapsack at school. Then you'll know where it is all the time.

Keep your first set of plaster study casts (the ones with the crooked teeth and bad bite), or a photograph before braces (all smiles), where you can see it.

IT'S NOT TOO LATE

If you have a retainer and it doesn't fit anymore —for whatever reason—please see your orthodontist. The orthodontist can adjust the retainer or make you a new one. Don't try to wear a retainer that doesn't fit. It will hurt, and, quite frankly, it won't do any good. You may feel embarrassed about going to your orthodontist to have your retainer adjusted or replaced, but it's worth it. Don't let all the time, effort, and money spent in straightening your teeth go down the drain. It's a terrible waste.

Think of it this way. Your friend has lost fifty pounds of fat on a diet. He gains back five pounds. Should he become discouraged, say, "What the heck!", and gain the other forty-five pounds back? Wouldn't you advise your friend to hold his weight at the five-pounds-extra line—or even encourage him to lose the five extra pounds again?

So your teeth have drifted back a bit. Let's hold the line there, and not lose all the benefit of your hard work.

You did it, now keep it!

"Now that your braces are off, how do you feel?" This was my final question to kids who were finished with their orthodontic treatment when I interviewed them. Sixteen-year-old Nancy spoke for most of them: "It took me two weeks or so to get used to my teeth. I couldn't be pulled away from a mirror for days. Now I have almost perfect teeth and I won't have problems with them later on."

A surprising number mentioned that they missed their braces at first. Tommy, a tenth-grader, told me, "My braces are off. All I could say when they came off was, 'Thank goodness,' but then it was like I was missing something from my mouth that belonged to me. You get attached to them!"

Whatever your response is when your braces finally come off, be sure to keep your straight teeth in top condition. Follow these rules for good dental health:

Eat a balanced diet.

Avoid sugar.

Brush and floss correctly and regularly.

Go to the dentist for checkups and cleanings every six months.

And *smile!*

Appendix:
A Short Short
History of Dentistry

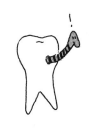

about 5000 B.C., *Euphrates River Valley*

A cuneiform tablet documents the tooth worm theory—that toothaches result from worms eating inside the mouth. This belief is strongly held until the early eighteenth century.

about 3000 B.C., *Egypt*

The Egyptians drain abscesses, treat periodontal disease, and make some false teeth.

about 25 A.D., *Rome*

Aulus Cornelius Celsus, a medical writer, recommends the use of finger pressure to straighten crooked teeth.

about 60 A.D., *Rome*

Pliny, a historian, refers to mechanical devices used to straighten teeth.

about 80 A.D., *Rome*

Cascallius becomes the first dentist to have his name preserved for history.

about 400–1500 A.D., *Europe*

Barbers and traveling groups of quacks practice unskilled dentistry at fairs and markets.

1728, *France*

Pierre Fauchard, often called the founder of modern dentistry, finally puts the tooth worm theory to rest and begins to raise dentistry from a trade to a profession. (His two-volume textbook on dentistry, *The Surgeon Dentist*, is still used today.)

1790s, *America*

Paul Revere practices dentistry. He identifies the body of Dr. Warren, a Revolutionary War hero, among bodies in a common grave by dental work he did for him years before.

1840, *America*

The first dental school in the world is established in Baltimore, Maryland.

1844, *America*

Nitrous oxide, or "laughing gas," is first used as a general anesthetic. (Up to this time, dental work was always done without anesthesia.)

1890, *America*

Edward Angle classifies the three types of malocclusion. A few years later he establishes a special school to teach orthodontics.

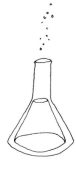

1905, *America*

Novocaine, a local anesthetic for dental patients, is developed.

1962, *America*

Scientists develop an adhesive that bonds metal and plastic brackets directly to teeth.

1972, *America*

Nitinol, an extremely flexible space-age metal that can "remember" shapes, is first used for archwires.

Suggestions for Further Reading

Hold, Robert Lawrence. *Straight Teeth: Orthodontics and Dental Care for Everyone.* New York: William Morrow & Co., 1981.
   A guide to orthodontics for older adolescent and adult readers. This book describes orthodontics in the context of complete dental care. For example, brushing, flossing, tooth nutrition, and fluoride treatment are discussed under "Prevention and Early Treatment." Includes a thorough discussion of orthodontic treatment for adults. Illustrated with drawings. Glossary.

Silverstein, Dr. Alvin, and Silverstein, Virginia B. *So You're Getting Braces: A Guide to Orthodontics.* New York: J. B. Lippincott, 1978.
   Directed to the young patient. Clear explanations of orthodontic procedures are illustrated with references to the orthodontic case studies of the authors' children. The book is generously illustrated with drawings and with photographs documenting the Silverstein children's treatment. Written for the young adolescent reader, but parents will also find it instructive.

Weiss, Jay, D.M.D. *Embraceable You.* New York: Health Sciences Publishing, 1975.
   An orthodontist wrote this layman's guide to orthodontics for the older adolescent and adult reader. Solid information about orthodontics is laced with literary and historical references, dental and otherwise. Six center pages of drawings and photographs illustrate the text. Glossary of terms.

Index

Jeanne Betancourt has taught junior high and high school, has designed and taught courses in film and television, and has run workshops for librarians and educators on film programming for adolescents. She is president of New York Women in Film and is a contributing editor to *Channels* magazine. She is on the faculty of the Media Studies Masters' Program at the New School for Social Research and on the board of advisors of the Media Center for Children. Her published work includes articles, reviews, and book-length adaptations of two films for young people.

Ms. Betancourt, who had her teeth straightened as a teenager, lives in New York City. Her daughter, Nicole, currently wears braces.